First Time Dad

The Ultimate Guide for New Dads about Pregnancy Preparation and Childbirth - Advice, Facts, Tips, and Stories for First-Time Fathers!

Lyon Tyler

Contents

"Being a father helps me be more responsible. You see more things than you've ever seen."

– Kid Rock

Introduction

Congratulations! You are going to be a father! In about nine months, you will be bringing your brand new baby home. You are very excited, but also very scared! What does this new chapter in your life bring for you? Will you be a good father? What will your baby look like? How can you support your partner during the pregnancy? Are you prepared for childbirth? How do you change a baby? How do you feed a baby? What do pregnant mothers eat?

The questions are racing through your head during this very pivotal period of your life. You are a new father! It is to be expected. You are also very likely feeling vulnerable, anxious, and maybe even scared. Fatherhood is one of the biggest responsibilities you will ever hold in this lifetime – after becoming first choice quarterback at college, chief spider hunter, and POTUS! You want to give it as much attention and effort as you possibly can.

The one thing I can tell you is that we have all been there. We have all laid awake at night, next to our growing babies and pregnant partners, worried about what fatherhood holds for us. Our biggest worry is always, of course, "Will I be a great father and partner to my growing family?"

I am here to reassure you that you can with simple, everyday, common sense and a sprinkling of science. You wouldn't be reading this book if you did not appreciate the value of knowledge. I commend you on taking the first step towards becoming a great first-time father. Your eagerness to do what is right by reading this book is proof that you are on the right path! Congratulations!

In the past, fathers often ignored pregnancy in their partners, thinking it to be a "women's issue" alone. I am glad to say that we men are stepping up today to be involved in their child's lives during the entire pregnancy. Not only are men stepping up for the child, but they are also stepping up for mothers, happy to play a very active role in their new family. The ramifications of this new way of life are very encouraging.

Women no longer have to do it alone and fetuses can grow happily and healthily because mothers are getting enough support and care, reducing the amount of stress and negative emotions that mother and baby experience.

As we celebrate being better fathers, I must congratulate you on researching to be a great father and partner during pregnancy. Being a great father is not an unattainable goal that you can never reach! All you need is guided knowledge and the willingness and hard work to be one and the rest falls into place.

In this book, I will bring you all the information you need to know to prepare for pregnancy and childbirth. I will teach you all the essential information that each trimester of pregnancy brings, as well as how to look out for labor and how to devise a birth plan.

Lastly, I will bring you some much-needed advice on how to take care of your baby and your partner during the first couple of months post-birth! Rest assured that this book will take care of all your information needs so that you can continue to be excited about fatherhood. So, take time to decide on a name and to paint your baby's room. You deserve to enjoy this special moment of life.

I'm an online entrepreneur, author, and married full-time father of three children. After I met my wonderful wife at the age of 21, we got pregnant with our first ("surprise") son. Since that moment I fully committed myself to support my wife during pregnancy and childbirth, but I soon discovered that, while the "female world" was full of books and resources about pregnancy, we (dads-to-be) had to find our own way to be prepared.

It's an understatement to say that dad's skills did not come naturally. I had to learn them the hard way, so I could teach them to you the easy way. Here's how it happened: Early on, I figured out that I could learn these skills just like I studied for math or foreign language tests. I read everything I could get my hands on about what to expect—pregnancy & childbirth books, medical studies, and every parenting book ever written. Eventually, I attended courses on the subject. I also started a Facebook group of fathers with some friends.

On a whim, I decided to document all of my misadventures and takeaways as a human guinea pig in a journal. I began to discuss the information I collected with other groups of fathers. To my surprise and delight, I found I wasn't the only person concerned about this topic.

In our "lab", we endeavor to find the latest scientific studies and then turn them into real-life advice. We then share these strategies to ascertain their validity. In this way, each skill in this book has already been refined by thousands of dads who have used them in real-life situations.

Not unlike a husband to a pregnant wife, the book serves as an affable, funny, half-informed, well-meaning companion to the pregnancy books that do the real work. It brings you a much-needed balanced perspective that comes from real-world experience that I have had. In singular devotion to my subject, I have had two more children. My most recent child was born in 2016, an event that found me well-prepared. I can't lie! Every pregnancy is a unique adventure.

CHAPTER ONE

Looking Inwards

Did You Know?

Modern-day c-sections were invented in Sub-Saharan Africa, centuries before it was discovered by the rest of the world during the nineteenth century.

FROM THE VERY FIRST time your partner's pregnancy test shows positive, your life changes. You are now responsible for a life for the next eighteen years. I have no doubt you feel the lump forming in your throat at just the thought of that.

As a new father, you will have to take care of not only your baby but also your partner. You obviously want to be a great father. Who doesn't? You have dreams of being that great movie dad, who gets it right and looks perfect doing it! Picture The Rock in a fitted sweater! But the reality is often very different!

To be a good father, you don't need to be ripped like most leading Hollywood stars. I doubt your baby will care that their dad is a jacked superhero. What your baby really needs is for you to be a good person. It is not so different from all your other responsibilities if you have the right mindset. That is why I recommend that any new father focuses on their mindset first and foremost. You can be a good father if you understand that it all starts from within.

We men can sometimes be hesitant to look inwards. We have a "take charge" attitude, preferring to fix every problem as soon as it arises. Your daughter is kidnapped by the mafia and you hop on your Harley-Davidson to go rescue her. But what if, instead of guns, you needed to communicate with her kidnappers and show your vulnerable side?

You might as well learn now for when you need to rescue your baby!

Let me assure you that your new responsibilities are not a problem. They simply require a new "you" if you want to be a good father and partner. So what are the things you need to know to be a good first-time dad?

Putting Your Partner And Baby First

Many people believe that humans act out of self-preservation, which is just a nice way of saying that we are all selfish. When you are a parent, you have to make many sacrifices. You have to put your baby and your partner first in every decision you make. You may be tempted to think that this is easy. After all, you already do that? But how easy is it for you to put your baby first when you have to wake up for the sixth night in a row to rock them back to sleep even though you have to work the next day? How easy is it to put your partner first when you have to cancel your game with the boys to stay home with her during another bout of morning sickness? What if you want to buy that new game but your partner needs to buy some new maternity clothes?

You will need to give yourself regular pep talks. Breathe and calm down. Meditate for a few seconds and tell yourself that you can do this! Here is what basketball MVP, LeBron James says about determining to be the best that he can be:

> *"All my life I've been striving to make myself better. It's a full-time commitment. To be the best, you have to work the hardest. You have to chase what seems impossible over and over and over again, because giving up is not an option, and when you feel like you've reached your limit, it's only the beginning, that's when the time to dig deep, to find the courage to push some more, because if you've got the drive, the discipline, and the resolve to do what it takes to make yourself great, then the rewards are en dless."*

You will need to communicate honestly with your partner about the difference a baby will make to your life. You both need to look inwards at your relationship before the baby arrives. Whereas you and your partner spent time with each other regularly, you will no longer be able to do that for the first months after the baby's arrival.

Babies need constant, round-the-clock care. They are practically defenseless. They need you to burp them, bathe them, comfort them, feed them, watch over them and even change your baby's diaper many times over at night because they are fully soaked... didn't you know? Baby poops during the night too! They also need to be fed every one to three hours.

You and your partner will have a lot of broken sleep and sleepless nights, so you should discuss how you will share the work of parenting your baby before it comes. Who will work and who will stay home with the baby? Will you feed the baby in turns every other night so that you can get more sleep?

One out of five partners breaks up after their baby arrives (Rossiter, 2019). When you watch Hollywood movies, you see partners hugging the baby, smiling and kissing happily in the beautiful sunrise, their hair styled perfectly to fit with the beautiful piano music in the background. I have some news for you, however. This is only one part of the story! Yes, you and your beautiful family will take plenty of happy strolls in the sunset, but it takes hard work.

The romance may dry out for a while because many mothers struggle to get back to their natural mental and emotional state months after the baby. Sometimes for even more than a year. But if you are willing to put your partner and baby first, things will get easier after the first few months.

Taking care of your baby is time-consuming but you must still spend time with your partner. We can easily become strangers to people we love if we don't spend time with them. Prioritize date night, no matter what. Sometimes date night might just be the two of you sleeping in after dropping the baby off at your parents. Or it could be eating pizza in your stained clothes until your friend or babysitter brings the little terror back. Of course, I mean this as a joke... maybe!

Pregnancy is very traumatic for the mother and your partner may not feel like having sex at first. She will need time to recover her physical, emotional, and mental health. You would too if you had to push out a football while your partner skates by not being able to comprehend how much pain you are in!

Put yourself in her shoes. Reassure her that you put her healing first and there is no pressure to return to your former sex life before the baby. Be empathetic and supportive of her. This will make her feel loved and she will be more emotionally open, honest and vulnerable with you.

On the other hand, men need love too. Sometimes, we want to be the small spoon! There will be times when you will need your partner to tell you how much of a great dad and partner you are. Don't be afraid to share this with her. Who doesn't like hearing words of praise from someone they love? You should both be encouraging and praising each other daily! I mean, you probably get big-headed when a coworker notices how good your new haircut looks. So a nice word from your partner will probably do a lot to lift your spirits - and vice versa!

I definitely encourage you to start building an open relationship with your partner now. It will help you work through conflicts with your partner much quicker once the baby arrives. Imagine trying to deal with a conflict calmly and respectfully when you have only slept for four hours in three days!

Building an open relationship now will also prepare you to address conflicts in your relationship once the baby arrives. When you are both sleep-deprived and your baby won't stop crying, it can be very easy to get into an argument with each other. Talk about how you will handle it before the baby arrives.

For example, you may decide that you will both give each other a few minutes break when you start to take out your frustrations on each other. You may decide to reconnect once the break is over by saying love-affirming words to each other like: "I am glad you are here to support me."

In some cases, you may be having problems with your partner. Perhaps you cannot see eye to eye and are fighting all the time. Seek therapy together if this is the case. If a baby can pick up on its mother's negative state even in the womb, think about how much all the negative energy will affect your child once it is born. In fact, scientists have found that high stress increases the level of the hormone, cortisol in a pregnant woman's system. If sufficient enough, these cortisol levels can affect the fetus' brain negatively.

Chronic and common life stressors in a pregnant mother can lead to "mixed handedness, autism, affective disorders, and reduced cognitive ability" in fetuses (Kinsella & Monk, 2013). No stress, no fights, and happy parents equal a happy, healthy baby.

Taking Care Of Your Mental Health

All the pep talks in the world will not work if you are not physically and psychologically healthy. Think of your favorite sports personality. What do they pay attention to the most? Their body and mind. As Muhammad Ali said: "float like a butterfly, sting like a bee!" You have to get into the ring ready to win the belt of fatherhood. Be healthy and the rest will follow. Lucky for you, there are many ways to take care of your health. Be aware of any changes from how you normally feel. If your emotions or physical health are starting to interrupt your day-to-day life, talk to your partner's GP, obstetrician, or midwife – the earlier the better.

You should also be careful what you read about pregnancy and fatherhood. Some websites and articles might make you feel worse or give you bad information. Always look at the source of what you read or consume. Can you trust the source of the information? Can you find other reputable sources that say the same thing?

Don't be afraid to ask questions when you and your partner visit specialists. No question is too stupid, perhaps apart from, "How do I tell if the baby is a boy or a girl when it arrives?" Asking questions also has another advantage: your partner will feel supported knowing that you are taking an active interest in the pregnancy.

Challenge yourself every day! Now that you are going to be a father, maybe you want to take up a hobby to improve your mind. You want your child to think you are the most intelligent father in the world! So read more books and watch more documentaries. You can decide to solve more puzzles or even start that business you have always dreamed of. Taking care of your brain health also incorporates eating food that is good for your brain, such as oats, turmeric, nuts, eggs, foods rich in vitamin c, such as oranges and fatty fish (Jennings, 2021).

Taking Care Of Your Physical Health

Regular exercise is a great way to boost your mental health and physical health. It makes you look good and even gives you a chance to meditate. Exercise drastically reduces your risk of chronic diseases which is a great benefit

(Warburton et al., 2006). As a new father, you want to be as healthy as you can for your baby. You can't have fun taking your baby on a walk if you get out of breath too easily. And you can't take care of your family if you are spending all your time battling a health concern.

In addition, your partner will feel better knowing that you are in great health. Plus, exercising has the side benefit of making you look good, helping to keep things spicy in the bedroom.

Former Mr. Universe and ex-governor of California, Arnold Schwarzenegger said: "Training gives us an outlet for suppressed energies created by stress and thus tones the spirit just as exercise conditions the body." There are so many ways to exercise that you will find one that works for you. Yoga, pilates, basketball, running, swimming, lacrosse, cycling, and more will help you get some much-needed time alone. You can clear your head, feel good and return to your family with a bright smile on your face.

High-intensity exercises, like running and cycling, have been found to produce the greatest benefits all around. I also recommend regular stretching exercises to help you reduce and manage your stress (American Council On

Exercise, 2014). Regular stretching keeps you flexible and exercise increases your stamina, which is great for playing with your baby (and playing with your partner).

Don't be tempted to skip exercise just because you feel you don't have time. If you have friends and family who can take care of your baby while you exercise, then don't hesitate to ask for their help. You and your partner should share your schedules daily so that you can plan out alone time for yourselves each day. Daily time spent alone will help keep the peace between you and your partner too.

Don't neglect your diet either. The best predictor of great health is your diet. Our diets affect every aspect of our lives. For instance, a man trying to conceive will increase his fertility by eating foods high in zinc, omega-3 fatty acids, and folic acid (Stork OTC, 2021). You will be taking care of your partner during her pregnancy, so you will need to eat healthy food to improve your mental ability, focus, and your energy.

Eat complex carbohydrates like wholewheat, brown rice, and oats. Other foods that give you energy include olive oil, chickpeas, bananas, oatmeal, beets, and eggs (Migala, 2021). Drastically reduce or completely cut out sugar and simple carbohydrates like pizza and candy. This will also decrease your risk of early mortality, giving you peace of mind that you will be around for your baby for a very long time. Drink plenty of water too, to improve mental alertness and to keep your physical health in great shape.

If you have not done so, you should also see your doctor for a physical check-up. Make yearly checkups into a yearly or biannual practice. You want to catch any illnesses as early as possible before they do too much damage. If you have a family history of a particular illness, let your doctor know so they can monitor you closely.

How Do You Feel?

How do you feel? Despite all the changes in gender identity that we have seen in the past few decades, old gender stereotypes persist: men do not have emotions. And if we do, we never show it. We do not let our emotions get the better of us. We stifle it deep down to make sure that we can be a solid shoulder for everyone else around us. We do not rely on others to support us when we are going through very emotional periods in our lives.

Being a father will change how you deal with your emotions. Babies cannot regulate their emotions so, when your baby comes, you will need to be in touch with your feelings. You will also need to be able to regulate your emotions for your partner's sake. Women go through a rollercoaster of rapidly changing emotions during pregnancy.

Your partner will feel more supported knowing that she has a stable, emotional center ready to listen to her and validate her emotions. She will need someone to verbally and physically comfort her once in a while.

Your emotional health is very important. It is the one aspect of your life where you need to be selfish once in a while. Think of your emotional health as an inner well. You need that well to support you. You will notice that when that well is empty you feel "rundown" and unable to give others your emotional support and care. If you consistently feed your family from that well without taking the time to refill it, then you will soon run out.

For your family's sake, you will need to take time to yourself regularly to restore your emotional center and refill your well. Take time to do things that made you happy and fulfilled pre-pregnancy.

Let me be honest with you, knowing that you are expecting will bring up a lot of uncomfortable emotions that you may not want to explore. Let's face it guys, many of us grew up with fathers who were not emotionally present for us. We remember how much we wished he would just be open enough for us to feel loved and validated. Certainly, you don't want to do the same to your beautiful baby, brand new and bursting with life?

I battled with my feelings during the first few months of my partner's pregnancy. My father provided for us financially but he did not believe that a "good man" shows his emotions. He never told me he loved me and he never hugged me. In the end, I saw how lonely my father's actions made him. Towards the end of his life, he wanted to reach out but didn't even know how after so many decades of shutting himself away from everyone.

I wanted to break that cycle because I carried the hurt of not feeling loved by my father for many, many years. I did not want my baby to ever have to deal with the same pain. It reminded me of this quote by former US President, Barack Obama: "Someone once said that every man is trying to live up to his father's expectations or make up for their father's mistakes."

Becoming a new father will, no doubt, have you looking back on your relationship with your father. If it was a positive relationship filled with love and care, this would be a happy time for you to explore how to pass down that love to your baby. However, if your relationship with your father was, and still is, complicated, a part of you may feel hurt, anxious, and saddened about the news of your partner's pregnancy. You will begin to wonder if you can be a good dad to your child when your father never gave you an example of what a great father is.

I encourage you to talk these feelings out with your partner and let her know that you need her reassurance. After all, she wouldn't be having your baby if she didn't think you would make a good father? I also encourage you to seek counseling or therapy if you find these feelings overwhelming

It is common for men to struggle to deal with pregnancy. It is a particularly difficult time because it changes your relationship with your partner. You might be feeling neglected or rejected by your partner because she is focused on the pregnancy. You may be feeling anxious or depressed or empty. Many men feel jealous or angry at the lack of attention they get. It is particularly difficult because men have traditionally been left out of pregnancy, so you might feel like there is no place for you.

Don't ignore these feelings because they will only get worse the longer you ignore them. Some men find it helpful to pursue therapy to get in touch with their deeper emotions. If you are not able to afford therapy or find a government-sponsored therapist, then you can try to find a free hotline, where you can speak to someone who will listen to you without judgment. There are many great resources online for first-time fathers that will greatly help you. You just need to search for them.

Another form of support for expectant fathers is other fathers. Perhaps you are feeling unsure and uncertain. You may even feel as though you do not want the baby. These are all normal feelings and should not be repressed. It is easy to feel pressured to fake excitement when all you see are pictures of smiling fathers on all the websites you visit. Speaking with other fathers who have been through the same thing will help you sort through your feelings and feel much better.

If you want to be a good role model for your baby and a better partner, I recommend you look inwards to find emotional healing and stability. Still, change is painful and can disrupt relationships. While you are doing the work of looking inwards, your partner may notice that you do not seem as enthusiastic as she imagined you will be. Be honest and reassure her that you are here for her and love her, but you still need to work through your feelings so that you can be fully present for her.

Conceiving A Baby (For Those Trying)

If you are currently trying for a baby, you may be feeling anxious or worried about why you are not pregnant yet. For some people, conceiving is as simple as ABC. When you look at those people it can be hard to keep faith that you will get pregnant. After all, if it is so easy for others, why isn't it easy for you?

Typically, doctors do not consider you infertile until after a year of you unsuccessfully trying for a baby (or six months if your partner is 35-years-old or older). So, if it has been only a few months, you don't need to worry. All you need to do is be happy and enjoy this time with your partner, ensuring that she is happy too.

The happier and less stressed you are, the more likely you are to conceive a child. Even if your partner is infertile, there are many options out there for you. According to the CDC, 10 percent of women in the US between the ages of

15 and 44 have considerable difficulty getting pregnant so, rest assured, you are not alone (OASH, 2019). You have the option to change your lifestyle and diet to improve your fertility. You also have the option of in vitro fertilization (IVF), artificial insemination, medicines, surrogacy, and even adoption or fostering. Nowadays, fertility issues should not stop anyone from having a baby.

Never Give Up!

Once you begin the process of looking inwards, you will start to fill your "well." You will feel more excited and ready to prepare for the actual arrival of your baby. So how do you prepare for a baby and how do you take care of a pregnant partner? It can be a lot of work, but you can do this! Never give up!

CHAPTER TWO

Looking Outwards

Did You Know?

The more social support a mom has, the heavier (and healthier) her baby tends to be!

ONCE YOU BEGIN THE process of looking inwards, you will also need to begin looking outwards. Looking outwards means taking care of your partner, your baby, and your home. There is a lot of preparation that you must do during the early stages of pregnancy.

It may seem overwhelming, but putting things into lists will help you feel less overwhelmed. It will also help you manage your home as best as you can and give you a sense of purpose as you try to find your emotional center and take care of your inner world too.

During the first trimester of pregnancy, the idea of having a baby is not yet "real". You know that you are having a baby, but you cannot see it and it is not due for a while yet. In fact, most women do not begin to show (that is when their pregnancy bellies begin to poke out) at the beginning of the second trimester.

Hence, you may feel as though you don't need to do much around the house yet. However, time flies quickly during pregnancy and you will find yourself ill-prepared for the arrival of your baby if you don't begin in the first trimester.

How to Take Care Of A Pregnant Woman

Before diving into the type of diet and changes you should expect in your partner (see **Chapter Three**), you need to understand how to meet your partner's needs so that you can keep mother and baby healthy and happy.

The more emotionally healthy and centered you are as a father, the more successful you will be in taking care of your partner. Discussions of fatherhood often leave out the emotional side of being a father, as we have discussed in **Chapter One**. But, pregnancy is a very emotional state for everyone involved. It brings many instances when you will feel very vulnerable, such as when your partner begins to have hormonal swings when you witness the birth of your child or the first kick.

During my partner's pregnancy, I certainly had my moments of feeling as though my breath was knocked out of me. It was an experience that nobody could have prepared me for. I felt honored to watch the miracle of life being created and I gained a newfound respect for women who hold the key to life and take one for the team with so much courage and determination.

By being centered, you will be able to handle these moments with strength for you and your partner. In the past, this was not a responsibility that was expected of men. Men were not even allowed into the hospital room during childbirth! Now, we know better. We know that your partner will feel happy if she knows you are there to meet her emotional needs. Remember, happy mother, happy baby!

Another way to take care of a pregnant woman is to just be there emotionally. Offer her your presence. If she needs help cooking dinner because she is too tired, she will really appreciate you making dinner for her. If she is dealing with mood swings, thanks to changes in her hormones, then offer her your company and understanding without reacting with anger or frustration. (Make sure you practice self-care, such as exercising and meditating that will help you let go of your own negative emotions in a safe space. See **Chapter One.**)

Pregnancy is very difficult for women. The myth that it is a magical time of motherly wonder is only one part of reality. Indeed, for many women, pregnancy can be tough. Your support and your presence will give her the comfort to carry on even when she is frustrated or anxious. If your partner is going through mood swings, you will be happy to know that they pass quite quickly. You will be under fire for only a very short period, as mood swings typically tend to fizzle out just as quickly as they began.

As well as mood swings, some pregnant women deal with antepartum depression, which is a mood disorder very similar to clinical depression. If you see signs of depression in your partner, then alert her doctor immediately. Your doctor will be able to recommend a support group or a private psychotherapist. There is also the option of medication and therapy for your partner.

You should also try to create memories with your partner. This is a special time in your life that you will never get back again. More importantly, this is the last time you will have to spend time together with just two members of your family. Once your baby arrives, you will forever have three members in your family. While this will always be a great addition, you will never get those two-member moments back, at least not until your child becomes an adult, so enjoy it while it lasts. Do things you enjoy doing as a couple while you still have the chance.

Lastly, you want to be there physically for your partner. When she needs someone to drive her to her yoga class or hold her hand during regular checkups, you want to be there for her. Your partner will need plenty of massages, baths drawn, errands to find the food she is craving at midnight, and so on.

You will need to have the patience of a snail running a marathon. Think of it as practice for fatherhood, where your patience levels need to be almost godly! Remember that you are also trying to build a good foundation with your partner and baby for the rest of your days. This is a perfect way to start. In the past, pregnant women were always doted on and cared for by the entire village exactly because they are in a very vulnerable state and need support. Your partner does not have a whole village, but she has you!

Being there for your partner physically and emotionally is what will get you to form a healthy and close relationship with her. Your baby will tie you to your partner indefinitely, so cultivating a good relationship with her promotes a healthy, happy family. This is, of course, a big responsibility, but it is a doable one!

Preparing Your Home For Your Baby's Arrival

There are not many parents that will admit to you that they ever left their baby unsupervised for even just one moment. But here is the big secret: every parent has. We all have that story about the time our babies fell or our babies put something in their mouths they really shouldn't, or got their hands on some products that they shouldn't have. At that moment, you panic and you consider all the ways in which you are a terrible, awful parent who does not deserve this wonderful, chubby baby.

Becoming a parent does not turn you into Superman overnight. You are still human and prone to mistakes. This is why you need to prep your house to turn it from a baby death trap into a safe haven for your chubby wonder. Of course, you will do your best to never leave your baby unsupervised. but babies are sneaky and they are fast when they want to cause trouble! They are very curious and will use any opportunity they can find to explore their surroundings. Always remember this anonymous quote that says: "A toddler can do more in one unsupervised moment than most people can do all day."

Here is how to prep your home for your baby's arrival:

- If you don't already have one, install a landline phone that works even when the electricity is down - in case of emergencies. Purchase a few mobile phone power banks and keep them charged at all times. Keep two written lists of your emergency contacts: one at home and one at work.

- Place knives and all sharp objects inside locked drawers. If your drawers do not have locks, use magnetic baby locks.
- Place all toxic or hazardous materials on very high top shelves. Alternatively, place them on bottom shelves that are securely locked.
- Install baby gates at strategic points throughout the house, for example at the top and bottom of stairs and the kitchen and bathroom doorways.
- Place non-slip mats underneath your rugs and at the entrance of tiled areas, like the kitchen and bathroom.
- Add finger-pinch guards to the hinges of your doors.
- Remove choking hazards on your door stops.
- Place all medication in a high cabinet where your baby cannot reach.
- Remove coffee tables and other such tables, side furniture, and house accessories, like vases and lamps. For furniture that you have to keep in the room, make sure they have no sharp edges. If they do, remove it! Some parents like to add safety padding on sharp furniture edges but your baby can accidentally pull them off or they could accidentally come off without you realizing it.
- Store all electrical appliances away unless you need them. As soon as you are through with them, put them

away securely on a high shelf. Do not leave electrical appliances out and about, especially plugged in.

• Ensure that big furniture items, like wardrobes, are firmly and safely rooted to the ground. If they are wobbly, remove them immediately. For the rest, secure them to the wall to ensure they won't fall even if the baby is leaning or pushing on them.

• Remove any electrical appliance with electric cords. For any that you cannot remove, place the cords tied together and hidden so that your baby cannot chew on it or trip on it.

• Cover up heating vents and radiators.

• Remove any blinds that use cords. If you have very long curtains that your baby can reach from the floor, replace them with shorter curtains that your baby cannot reach.

• Put baby-proof safety covers on all electrical outlets.

• Research every plant in your house. Give away toxic varieties and ensure you only buy non-toxic ones with a baby in the house.

• Remove any hanging clothes, for instance, hand towels in the kitchen and bathroom or tablecloths on your dining table.

• Add knob covers on all the knobs of your oven. Place hob covers on the hob and only cook using the back hobs so your baby will not be burned if it touches the front hobs. If you use a gas cooker, I strongly suggest you replace it with an electrical one if you can.

• Place fire extinguishers and first aid kits in as many rooms as you can, particularly the nursery, bedroom, kitchen, and living room. Install smoke detectors as well as carbon monoxide alarms in every room in your house.

• Research the best baby cribs and nursery furniture that comply with national regulations. These regulations are put in place to keep your baby safe. For example, the crib may need to be fire retardant as may your baby's blankets, mattress, clothes, and so on.

• Purchase a good thermometer to check the temperature of the water is just right for the baby's baths.

• Add a toilet lock to toilet lids.

• Remove cosmetics on bathroom counters and sinks and place them in a high cabinet.

• Vacuum regularly because babies love to put things they find on the floor in their mouths.

Financial Planning

If you went to a broker and asked them to make an investment where you are guaranteed to lose money, you would rightfully be called crazy. Having a baby is an investment, just not a financial one. In fact, you are certain to lose a lot of money as soon as you receive the news that you are pregnant. Hospital visits are not free. Baby clothes, unfortunately, are not free. Neither are diapers, the baby's medical check-ups, and daycare costs. What's more, you are not paid for all the time you take off work to take care of your baby.

As much as a great emotional investment having a baby is, you cannot support this investment without relying on good finances. Likewise, it is not fair to bring a baby into this world if you cannot give it the financial resources needed to thrive and succeed. When financial planning the one question to ask yourself is this: "Do I have enough to support my baby for the next few years into adulthood?"

While it is not possible to say you have enough on you presently, you should be able to stand proudly and say that you can continue to make enough to take care of your child's finances. Perhaps this is through your educational achievements, which means you stand a better chance of holding down a good job. Or, maybe you have good financial investments that you hope will give good returns. You may have your own business, which you can work at to make sure you have financial freedom. Even without these things, you can make it work.

As of June 2021, the cost of raising a child until they turn eighteen years old is $284,570. This figure is specific to the United States and may be higher or lower depending on which country you reside. However, you can tell that raising a child is seriously expensive. And this figure does not include financially supporting your child through college or university.

You need disposable income, a stable job, good insurance coverage for health, death, and all other types of insurance that apply to you. You also need to have emergency funds that include up to six months of expenses and you need to be in a position where you are regularly saving for retirement.

Your expenses should cover things like rent, mortgage, and any unforeseen circumstances in your child's life. They will cover the cost of sharing experiences and building good memories with your baby, for example going on vacation together. These are times for bonding as well as getting away from the day-to-day pressures of life.

Finally, you need to be able to save for college or university so that your child has less financial burden in young adulthood and can get a good education to plan for their own financial future. For many parents, this comes in the form of opening a savings account for their child.

You will need to add your baby to your health insurance coverage as soon as it is born. You should also make a will and keep it regularly updated for your baby's benefit.

To avoid getting into debt, ensure all your bills are placed on a standing order or direct debit payment plan. All you will need to do is ensure you have enough money in your account(s) each month to cover your payments.

If all this sounds quite daunting, don't worry. These things won't all come at once. The majority of dads-to-be don't know how they are going to fund such a large commitment, but they do. And that is the key word – commitment. Stick at it, through thick and thin and you will be fine.

There are several online calculators that will help you estimate how much it would cost you to raise your child. Themeasureofaplan.com has a good infographic guide to help you do this for your individual circumstances.

CHAPTER THREE

What To Expect In The First Trimester

Did You Know?

Babies can start crying in the womb from as early as 28 weeks.

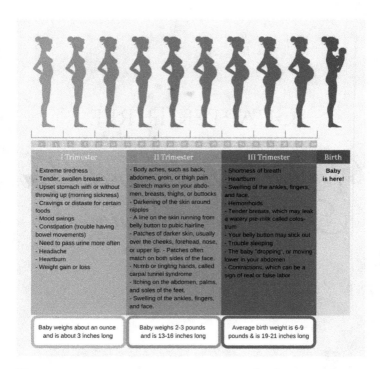

I Trimester	II Trimester	III Trimester	Birth
- Extreme tiredness - Tender, swollen breasts. - Upset stomach with or without throwing up (morning sickness) - Cravings or distaste for certain foods - Mood swings - Constipation (trouble having bowel movements) - Need to pass urine more often - Headache - Heartburn - Weight gain or loss	- Body aches, such as back, abdomen, groin, or thigh pain. - Stretch marks on your abdomen, breasts, thighs, or buttocks - Darkening of the skin around nipples - A line on the skin running from belly button to pubic hairline - Patches of darker skin, usually over the cheeks, forehead, nose, or upper lip. - Patches match on both sides of the face. - Numb or tingling hands, called carpal tunnel syndrome - Itching on the abdomen, palms, and soles of the feet. - Swelling of the ankles, fingers, and face.	- Shortness of breath - Heartburn - Swelling of the ankles, fingers, and face. - Hemorrhoids - Tender breasts, which may leak a watery pre-milk called colostrum - Your belly button may stick out - Trouble sleeping - The baby "dropping", or moving lower in your abdomen - Contractions, which can be a sign of real or false labor	Baby is here!
Baby weighs about an ounce and is about 3 inches long	Baby weighs 2-3 pounds and is 13-16 inches long	Average birth weight is 6-9 pounds & is 19-21 inches long	

THE FIRST TRIMESTER IS notorious for being very unpleasant and uncomfortable for the mother. It is the trimester where the mother suffers morning sickness, is often unable to keep food down, and suffers from little sleep. Chicago Tribune writer, Lauren Chval (2017) describes her very unpleasant experience with the first trimester:

"Pop culture representations and mythic understandings of pregnancy had misled me.

"Of course, I'd heard of morning sickness, but apart from that pesky aside, I was under the impression that pregnancy was an amazing time in a woman's life. 'magical' seems to be the word most often used. You have a glow about you. You're a goddess of fertility. Your body is doing what it is meant to do (they say almost threateningly).

"The most shocking betrayal of my naive conception of pregnancy was the first ultrasound. TV shows had led me to believe that cold goo is squirted onto your belly and then the doctor moves the wand around your skin to reveal the baby on the screen. Not so! When the fetus is that small, the wand is inserted into the vagina to capture the image. It is no more pleasant than it sounds.

"At that moment, I couldn't help but feel a kernel of resentment toward my husband as he sat opposite me, staring at the screen with the faintest hint of tears in his eyes. He was seeing our baby for the first time as a wholly positive experience, unburdened by the discomfort of having a machine thrust inside his body. For him, this was magical...

"That mental barrier between my husband and me persisted throughout the first trimester. I was plagued by nausea and headaches that made me cry. I woke up to pee every

single night. Worst of all was the crushing exhaustion...
There were two of us inhabiting my body now, but I felt
isolated. It wasn't the experience I'd been promised."

As a new father, you might be worried about how to take
care of your partner during such an uncomfortable first
trimester. This chapter will teach you all the things you
need to know about the first trimester so that you can best
help your partner reduce her discomfort and frustration.
So what should you expect during the first trimester? If
you do feel overwhelmed or as though you are not doing
a good job, stop to breathe and remind yourself that you
are trying your best and, scientifically, this is already giving
your partner and baby a great start. Once calm, then you
can focus on improving and being the best father that you
can be!

As world-renowned survival expert Bear Grylls said:
"Survival can be summed up in three words - never give
up. That's the heart of it really. Just keep trying."

Fetal Growth

The **first two weeks** of a woman's period are counted
as part of her pregnancy, even though conception typically

begins two weeks after a woman's period - during ovulation.

During ovulation and conception, between **weeks three** and **four**, Ovulation occurs when an egg is released in anticipation of being fertilized. If there is any sperm in the woman at the time (sperm can survive inside a woman's uterus for up to three to five days after sex) it fertilizes her eggs and conception begins during week three. The fertilized egg forms what is known as a zygote. In some cases, it can form two zygotes (twins) or three zygotes (triplets) or more. Usually, multiple zygotes are formed either because the fertilized egg divides, leading to identical twins, triplets, and so on, or because multiple eggs were released and fertilized by different sperm, leading to non-identical twins, triplets, and more.

By **week four**, the zygote travels through the fallopian tube, implanting itself in the uterus. It begins to form its amniotic sac. By **week four**, the amniotic sac is formed and an embryo begins to grow inside the sac. As soon as the amniotic sac forms, it fills with amniotic fluid which is made up of the mother's plasma, nutrients, hormones, and antibodies. The fluid protects your embryo in the womb. The placenta also begins to form in **week four**.

The placenta is an incredibly important organ that keeps your baby alive. In fact, many miscarriages in the first trimester occur because the placenta did not develop properly. The placenta allows oxygen, blood, and nutrients to travel between mother and baby. It also transfers waste from the baby to the mother, who then expels this waste.

By **week five** the mother's body will begin to notice that she is pregnant because of an increase in the hormone, human chorionic gonadotropin (hCG). When a woman takes a home pregnancy test, those tests read for increased levels of hCG. The mother's body will now begin to produce more progesterone, which is responsible for other biological processes like lactation and enabling the placenta to grow. An increase in progesterone also causes an increase in estrogen, another important hormone for pregnant mothers. The umbilical cord will now begin to take shape in **week five**.

By **week six**, the embryo still looks like a happy half-toad, half-dolphin hybrid! It is as small as a pea and could sit very comfortably in your palms. The organs begin to form and the spine forms that C-shape you see in embryo pictures. The structures where eyes, ears, and arms will form also now begin to form, with buds forming where the arm will grow. By **week seven**, the embryo's retinas begin to form, and the brain begins to develop. The structures where nostrils and legs will form also now begin to form.

By **week eight**, all the body parts already mentioned continue to develop while the nose finishes forming. The embryo now officially becomes a fetus. The upper lip begins to form and the neck begins to straighten. The arm buds have turned into paddles and fingers now begin developing there. The leg buds also now begin turning into paddles. while the eyes and retinas begin to develop more complexity. It is now about the size of a raspberry, between 0.5 to 0.6 inches long from the top of the head to the rump. By **week nine**, the fetus is about the size of a cherry. It slowly begins to look more human-like and is about 0.6 to 0.7 inches long.

By **week ten** the toes and fingers are fully formed and the fetus can now bend its elbows. It is about an inch long. By **week eleven**, genitalia begins forming and the eyes separate, with the fetus reaching two inches, about the size of a brussel sprout. By **week twelve** the fetus stops looking like a dolphin-hybrid and begins to look more human because the face has formed fully. It will measure about 2.5 inches in length, about the size of a passion fruit. Moving on to the next week, **week thirteen**, the fetus' kidneys and other organs are now fully formed, even though it is only about the size of a plum, at about 3 inches. You are now moving towards your second trimester by this week.

Mother's Health and Body

Encourage your partner to exercise. You can join her for walks, swims, prenatal yoga, or light weight lifting in the gym to encourage her to exercise. Having sex is also a great way for both of you to trigger the release of feel-good hormones while you also exercise and destress. It is perfectly safe during the first trimester, as long as you try not to place any weight or pressure on her belly.

For some women, hormonal changes cause them to have a much lower libido. For other women, the opposite occurs. Some women confess that their fuller figures give them more sexual confidence, leading them to initiate more sex with their partner. Nevertheless, sex during pregnancy can be dangerous if your partner is carrying twins, triplets, or more or if she has a history of miscarriage. If either of you have sexually transmitted diseases, then you should avoid sex to avoid infecting your baby.

Pregnant mothers in the first trimester often feel sleepy and tired, to the point of fatigue and exhaustion. Their bodies are not used to the hormonal changes and the pregnancy, so it affects their energy levels. Keep the house clean and calm so that she feels relaxed.

Then there is the dreaded and notorious morning sickness and nausea. Some pregnant women are lucky because it does not affect them. However, four out of five pregnant women suffer from this symptom. It is not a cause for concern unless she is not able to keep any food or drinks down; is throwing up more than five times a day, and has lost more than five percent of her normal weight before pregnancy.

A pregnant woman suffering from morning sickness should try to eat smaller portions every couple of hours and sip water and other fluids slowly throughout the day. Fried and fatty foods trigger vomiting, so these should be avoided. She should also avoid extreme weather temperatures and wear loose, comfortable clothing. Your doctor will prescribe prenatal vitamins and folic acid to your partner at her first check-up. These vitamins will go a long way in ensuring that the baby's first-trimester development is healthy. Folic acid reduces her chances of a miscarriage and the baby's chances of birth defects. If your partner is not able to keep these vitamins and supplements down, however, then you must contact your doctor ASAP.

Other symptoms that show up in the first trimester are headaches and pain in the calves and legs. Headaches are common during the first trimester because of hormonal changes, low blood sugar from excessive vomiting, and tiredness from waking up all night due to frequent urination. Fatal headaches, on the other hand, are rare and are a sign that the mother has developed a blood clot in her brain. This usually happens if she has a familial history of blood clots. Blood clots are also able to develop in the legs or calves. When this happens, both body parts begin to ache severely and even swell.

UTIs are also quite common in pregnant women so she should visit her doctor immediately if she experiences a stinging pain while urinating. UTIs can be fatal to the fetus and need to be taken very seriously.

Another fatal symptom is heavy bleeding. This is different from mild bleeding, which is fairly common. Call emergency services immediately if your partner begins to bleed heavily as it is a symptom of either an ectopic pregnancy or a miscarriage, both of which are dangerous.

You should also call the doctor immediately if your partner is running a fever, has body aches, pain in the joints, rashes, difficulty breathing, or any other symptoms of flu or an infection. You can pretty much guarantee that if the mother gets something the baby will catch it too, and that can be fatal for one so small with no immune system yet.

Your obstetrician-gynecologist (OB-GYN) will alert your partner of all the symptoms to look out for and which ones can be deadly. Hence, it will be to your benefit to go to check-ups with your partner so you don't miss anything.

Food And Diet

A mother's diet contains most of the nutrients that the baby will need to grow healthily. It also contains all the ingredients needed to keep the mother healthy since pregnancy is very hard on a woman's body. The morning sickness, nausea, and heartburn that most women experience during pregnancy also make it difficult for mothers to keep their food down, especially during the first and third trimesters. She can eat a little at a time to prevent herself from getting nauseous, so try to prepare foods with the important nutrients needed for pregnant women.

The nutrients important during all three trimesters are:

NUTRIENT	FUNCTION	FOODS
Calcium	The fetus needs calcium to develop its teeth and bones. If the mother does not eat enough calcium, her body will get it by "stealing" it from her bones and teeth. Some women end up losing their teeth. Some women also become more likely to develop osteoporosis.	Dairy food and products, calcium-enriched orange juice, kale, sardines, salmon, tofu, leafy greens, and broccoli.
Chaoline	The fetus uses choline to develop a healthy brain and its cell membranes.	Eggs, broccoli, cauliflower, salmon, lean beef, and chicken.
Copper	Copper is used for the fetus' growth and development, including developing its heart, brain, bones, blood cells, blood vessels, connective tissues, and nervous, skeletal, and immune systems. It also gives the mother energy at a time when she is more tired than normal.	Cashews, hazelnuts, prunes, black pepper, crabs, sunflower seeds, cocoa, shitake mushrooms, and whole grains.
DHA (Docosahexaenoic acid)	DHA is a type of omega-3 fatty acid found mostly in the eyes and brain. That is why the fetus needs it for its visual and mental development. Make plenty of DHA-rich food during week 8 when the fetus' eyes are being developed with more complexity.	Sardines, fortified eggs, light canned tuna, and salmon. (Some other fish, like bigeye tuna and swordfish) contain DHA but can give your partner and fetus mercury poisoning, so avoid them.
Fiber	Fiber allows the food your partner eats (and the nutrients they contain) to move through her more easily, allowing the nutrients to get to all the organs that need them. It reduces your partner's chances of developing gestational diabetes by regulating her blood glucose levels. It also reduces her chances of developing preeclampsia and high blood pressure.	Whole grains, brown rice, whole-wheat pasta, lentils, quinoa, peas, broccoli, fresh fruits, beans, and bran.
Folic acid (vitamin B9) PART 1	You will have noticed that doctors prescribe folic acid to pregnant women. It is incredibly important for the fetus' development. Without enough folic acid, your baby's spinal cord, brain, heart, circulatory system, and red blood cells will not develop. Even more importantly, folic acid assists the body in creating DNA. Babies who do not get enough folic acid during their development tend to develop neural tube disorders like spina bifida. (The neural tube is what forms your baby's brain and spine.)	Fortified breakfast cereals, oranges, green leafy vegetables, beets, cauliflower, strawberries, kidney beans, and nuts.

Folic acid (vitamin B9) PART 2	Folic acid is needed the most during the first trimester because this is when most birth defects form. However, your partner will still need to consume folic acid to reduce her chances of preterm birth, heart defects, and gestational diabetes.	Fortified breakfast cereals, oranges, green leafy vegetables, beets, cauliflower, strawberries, kidney beans, and nuts.
Iodine	Your baby's brain and nervous system will not develop well without iodine. Without iodine, your baby might develop an intellectual disability. Your partner will need it for their thyroid, the gland that regulates her hormones core body functions and heart rate, body temperature, and metabolism.	Plain yogurt, eggs, shrimp, milk, cheddar cheese, iodized salt, baked cod, and light canned tuna.
Iron	This prevents your partner from feeling too tired since the baby is using a lot of iron to build its connective tissue.	Spinach, eggs, beef, chicken, beans, kale, and edamame.
Magnesium	It regulates every system in the baby and the mother's system. Without magnesium, the baby may develop preeclampsia or have poor fetal growth. The baby will also have weak teeth and bones.	Spinach, cashews, peanuts, black beans, edamame, avocado, peanut butter, kidney beans, and yogurt.
Manganese	It creates bone and cartilage for the fetus. It metabolizes all the cholesterol, amino acids, and carbohydrates that the mother eats so that the baby can use them to grow.	Brown rice, pecan nuts, oatmeal, pineapple, whole wheat bread, broccoli, carrots, legumes, peanuts, raisins, bananas, and whole grain.

Molybdenum	Molybdenum is only needed in very small quantities. The mother's body uses it to eliminate toxic chemicals from her body. Do not supplement with extra molybdenum because too much of it causes adverse health effects.	Kidney beans, lima beans, soybeans, black beans, garbanzo beans, barley, oats, dried peas, and lentils.
Omega-3 Fatty Acids	The baby uses omega-3 fatty acids to develop healthy eyes, brain, heart, and immune system. It is also very important during the third trimester when the baby's brain grows at its fastest rate. In addition, it prevents the baby from being born with low birth weight. They increase good cholesterol (HDL) and lower bad cholesterol (LDL) in the mother. They also reduce her blood pressure and help fight inflammation in her body. It will also help fight postpartum depression and reduce her mood swings.	Walnuts, cod, eggs, free-range chicken, light canned tuna, sardines, shrimp, crab, salmon, trout, walnuts, anchovies, flax seeds, and arugula.
Omega-6 Fatty Acids	The baby needs it to grow its bone, hair, and skin.	Brazil nuts, pine nuts, sesame seeds, vegetable oil, walnuts, pumpkin seeds, and almonds.
Phosphorus	It is used in most bodily functions.	Almonds, lentils, salmon, milk, eggs, peanuts, whole wheat bread, and yogurt.
Potassium	It helps organs function properly. It reduces muscle cramping in pregnant mothers, which is common during the third trimester.	Prunes, pears, oranges, dried apricots, lima beans, peanuts, wheat bran, bananas, carrots, sweet potatoes, and lentils.

Proteins	They are the building blocks of your fetus' muscles, skin, body, hair, and so on.	Poultry, cheese, milk, meat, nuts, yogurt, and beans.
Selenium	It synthesizes your baby's DNA and protects baby and mother against infections by strengthening the immune system.	Whole grain bread, brazil nuts, light canned tuna, turkey, chicken, lamb, and sardines.
Sodium	To help the muscles function properly.	Salt, plain yogurt, vegetables, milk, eggs, and grains.
Vitamin A, B1, B12, B2, B3, B5, B6, B7, C, D, E & K	Without vitamins, we all soon develop diseases because our bodies are not able to perform vital tasks that it needs to survive and stay healthy.	As many different varieties of fruit and vegetables as mama bear can eat, as well as dairy products, chicken, whole grain, mushrooms, and tuna.
Water	Like vitamins, water is required for every part of the body to function and for the health of the body.	Water, fruits, and vegetables.
Zinc	The baby will use it to create its DNA and to grow its cells. It prevents labor and birth problems during pregnancy and prevents low birth weight. Mothers also need it to improve their immune systems and prevent infection and illnesses.	Cashews, yogurt, baked beans, lean beef, dark turkey meat, meat, almonds, and peanuts.

Don't believe the myth that women are "eating for two" now. In fact, a pregnant woman in her first trimester typically has to eat only 2,000-2,100 calories a day, depending on her exercise level, her BMI, her height, how fast her metabolism is, and how many babies she is carrying. In the second trimester, this number moves up to 2,300-2,500 calories. Then, this increases to 2,600-2,800 calories a day in the third trimester.

These increases in calories just account for an increase in nutrients that your partner must eat. So, eating a bowl of strawberries might be better for dessert than a candy bar. The best part is that you can eat the same diet as your partner and you will see that you get healthy too. For any men who have a little bit of pregnancy belly going on, this might be a good way to lose that baby weight!

Pregnant women should avoid the following foods during pregnancy:

- Undercooked meat and poultry.
- Undercooked eggs.
- Raw fish.
- Raw shellfish.
- Certain fish, including swordfish, shark, bigeye tuna, orange roughy, king mackerel, and tilefish.
- Uncooked seafood.
- Too much caffeine.
- Alcohol.

- Unwashed fruits.
- Unwashed vegetables.
- Unpasteurized food.
- Herbal tea.

Your First Visit

As soon as you find out that you are pregnant, you should both book your first visit. This is where you will be prescribed multivitamins and folic acid and where you will be told of all the symptoms of ill-health to look out for.

The first test is always booked between weeks six and eight. It is natural for parents to feel nervous during the first check-up, especially first-time parents. A good OB-GYN will put you at ease and try to make your check-up as pleasant as possible.

The first thing your doctor will do is confirm that you are pregnant. Pregnancy test strips are accurate, but not 100 percent of the time. Once it is confirmed, your doctor will ask you and your partner a lot of questions about your health history (including your sexual health history) and your family's health history. This will help to pinpoint any health conditions that the baby may be at risk for. Finally, they will run the following tests:

- Pap smear: to check for cervical cancer.
- STD tests: to prevent your partner from transmitting the STD to the baby.
- Blood sugar test: if you or your partner have a familial history of diabetes, or if gestational diabetes runs in your partner's family.
- Urine test: to check your blood sugar levels, your protein levels, white blood cell levels, and your bacteria levels.
- Genetic carrier screening: to check you and your partner are not unknowingly carrying genetic conditions, such as Huntington disease, sickle cell anemia, or Tay-Sachs disease.
- Blood test: to ensure all your vitals are OK, as well as your vitamin and nutrient levels. Your blood work will also show if you are immune to various infections, like measles and it will help determine your blood type (if your doctor does not already have that on file).

Your doctor will be able to give you an expected due date for your baby at the end of your first visit. You will also be taught what foods to avoid and what foods to eat for a healthy pregnancy (see **Chapter Four**).

CHAPTER FOUR

What To Expect In The Second Trimester

Did You Know?

Your partner's heart grows bigger while she is pregnant, so do her feet. Her voice can change, her sense of smell can change and parts of her may change color.

THE SECOND TRIMESTER IS a breeze for most women. Nausea and morning sickness goes away and she starts to feel energized again. She can eat more and feel better and her hormones start to even make her feel happy. You will notice that she starts to have that "pregnancy glow" which really makes pregnant women look radiant and beautiful.

Since it is easier for her it will be easier for you too and you may even have more time to yourself during the second trimester. It is the best time for you to finish baby proofing the house and even take time for yourself! This is the perfect time for you to enjoy your last few moments of sleeping in because, from one father to another, once your little night terror arrives, you will forget what sleeping in feels like!

Your partner will start to show and her belly will start growing at really fast speeds. Even though the second trimester is generally easier than the first, your partner will still need plenty of foot and back massages because the growing baby will be placing a lot of pressure on this area. And while some women glow, some begin to experience skin issues in the second trimester. Here is one woman's experience of the second trimester:

"In the second trimester, I was able to say goodbye to the hormonal headaches I experienced in my first trimester. While my energy levels never fluctuated much, many women report feeling far more motivated and active as pregnancy hormones begin to level off and provide a more stable foundation for mums-to-be. Like many second-or-more-time-mums, compounded with the additional growth of baby number two, the physical changes of pregnancy came much thicker and faster than they did with my firstborn.

I continued to weight train throughout my second trimester, but cut high-impact exercises like jogging or jumping completely at this time. Subsequent pregnancies can prompt your center of gravity to shift faster, while muscle memory sees the joints and abdominal muscles give way more readily to the 'relaxing' effects of the pregnancy hormone relaxin.

I simplified my exercise selection, only practicing compound exercises (think squats, deadlifts, cleans, etc that use many muscle groups at once) with which I was very familiar. Sometimes that meant doing them in isolation rather than as part of a larger circuit, or simply reducing the weight I was lifting. While I continued lifting about 80% of my pre-pregnancy weight throughout my second trimester during my first pregnancy, 70% felt challenging and enjoyable enough this time around."

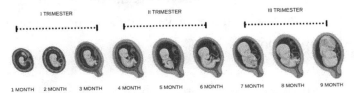

EMBRYONIC DEVELOPMENT

I TRIMESTER   II TRIMESTER   III TRIMESTER

1 MONTH 2 MONTH 3 MONTH 4 MONTH 5 MONTH 6 MONTH 7 MONTH 8 MONTH 9 MONTH

Fetal Growth

By **week fourteen** your baby's red blood cells now begin to form. This is the week where your baby will have almost fully developed their genitals. In some cases, the genitals are fully formed. Your baby now weighs about 1.5 ounces and measures about 3.5 to 4 inches from the crown of the head to the rump (buttocks), about the size of a nectarine. By **week fourteen**, the eyes now begin to move and the baby's sense of smell and taste begin to develop. The fetus looks even more human by now with the neck becoming defined. Most medical professionals also begin to measure babies above twelve weeks old with a crown-heel length as well as a crown-rump length.

By **week fifteen** the hair begins to grow slowly and the hair pattern begins to form. The lanugo will also begin to form. The lanugo is the downy, fine hair that covers the baby's entire body, but it disappears shortly after birth. The baby's heart begins to pump and the blood vessels start working and transporting red blood cells across the baby's body. The fetus is now about the size of a grapefruit, measuring about 4.5 inches.

By **week sixteen** the neck is defined enough to hold up the baby's head erect. Your baby can now move their arms and legs in coordinated movements. The ears have been lowering over the past couple of weeks and it can now hear what is going on in the outside world. The ultrasound may be able to pick out the baby's genitalia (and therefore sex) by this week. Your baby is about the size of an apple at **week sixteen**, about 4.6 inches, weighing 3.5 ounces.

By **week seventeen**, your baby begins to make fat tissue (called adipose). The fat cells begin to grow in the stomach walls, neck, breast, back, shoulders, arms, legs, chest, and face. This fat will fill out your baby's features. At the same time, the baby will now begin drinking from its amniotic fluid, practicing its sucking reflex. This reflex is what will help your baby to suckle and feed after birth. The umbilical cord is now increasing in length and volume, to provide more nourishment for the growing fetus. Your baby is now about the size of a pear, measuring about 5 inches and weighing 5 ounces.

At **week 18**, your baby starts to develop its own sleeping pattern as their internal clock begins to regulate. They will now cycle between sleep and being awake. You may now begin to feel flutters as your baby begins to move its limbs. These little kicks are known as "quickening." Quickening takes place between **week 18** and **week 20**. Adipose tissue will now also be developing on the toes and fingertips. Ultrasounds will be able to clearly pick up the baby's sex at this point. Your baby is now about the size of a sweet potato, measuring about 5.5 inches and weighing 7 ounces.

By **week 19**, your baby is now the size of a mango, measuring about 6.25 inches. The reproductive system is fully formed by now and the fingernails and toenails will begin to form too. The vernix caseosa will also now begin to form. If you have ever seen a childbirth, you will recognize the vernix caseosa as the white, waxy coating on the baby's skin when it is born. Think of the vernix caseosa as a protective layer keeping your baby's newly-formed skin from being damaged by the amniotic fluid. Without it, your baby's skin will become wrinkled or chapped from spending too much time in the amniotic fluid. Your baby is also more likely to catch an infection in the womb without the protection of this coating.

At **week 20**, your partner is halfway through her pregnancy. Your baby's sleep cycle is still developing. You may begin to notice that it is aware of the sounds in the surroundings. For example, they may start kicking when the room is noisy. During this week, some babies begin to suck their thumb as the sucking reflex develops. With the adipose tissues taking root in the face, your baby's features are becoming more pronounced. The brain is also developing at great speed and the meconium is now being formed too. This is the green-black substance produced by the digestive system as waste. It is the first bowel movement your baby will have after birth. Your baby is still tiny, at about the size of a bell pepper, measuring about 6.75 inches.

By **week twenty-one**, the toes and fingers are all formed, including fingerprints and toeprints. The digestive system is developing even though your baby is still receiving most of its nutrients from your partner. The bone marrow has now stepped up to the plate to produce red blood cells, giving the liver a well-deserved break. Your baby's eyelids are now beginning to separate in anticipation of its eyes opening. Your baby is about the size of a banana, with its crown-rump length measuring just over 7 inches.

Between **weeks twenty-two** and **twenty-four**, your baby is now sleeping eighty percent of the time in REM (rapid eye movement) sleep. The brain continues to develop and the eyes can now move, even though they are still shut. Your baby's sense of touch is now fully formed, as well as their eyebrows. Brown fat, which keeps us warm, now begins to develop too. Your baby is about the size of an eggplant, measuring between 7.5 inches to 8 inches and weighing between 15 to 20 ounces.

At **week twenty-fiv**e, the baby's nervous system and brain continue to develop. So too, the ears. Indeed, some babies begin to recognize voices by this week. I encourage you to talk to your baby, play music, read and introduce it to the outside world through sound. At this point it is about the size of an acorn squash, measuring about 10 inches.

The lungs and immune system are developing well by **weeks twenty-six** to **twenty-seven**. Hair is developing including head hair and eyelashes. Babies at this stage continue to suck their thumb, preparing for sucking once they are born. Your baby becomes more active, smiling and even opening its eyes finally. It now measures between 9 and 9.5 inches and weighs about 2 pounds and looks like a fully formed human, although there is still a lot more development to go, especially building up fat.

At this stage, if you shine a torch on your partner's belly, the baby will retreat because it can now see light and shadows. Speak to your baby often. Your voice is familiar and will comfort them. Your baby now

Mother's Health and Body

The mother's hormones start to level by the second trimester. She will start to feel much better and her appetite will begin to increase. Most of the negative changes to her body from the first trimester will now vanish or decrease significantly. However, the growing baby will now begin to stretch out the uterus, causing her pain at the sides of her body. As her uterus stretches, the ligaments in her lower stomach will also stretch to accommodate this growth. This may cause her some pain in her lower stomach too. Some women begin to see stretch marks because of the baby's rapid growth in the second trimester. In some cases, the linea nigra, a long dark line in the middle of the belly, will appear.

At the same time, even though her hormones have been regulated, they are still at a higher level than they would be in a non-pregnant woman. She may experience congested nose and nosebleeds. Her gums may also bleed too. Oftentimes this happens because her body begins to release a hormone called relaxin.

Relaxin causes the ligaments and joints in the body to loosen which, in turn, makes childbirth easier. Relaxin is also what causes women to have their infamous "duck waddle" walk during pregnancy, although I wouldn't advise you to call it that in her presence if you like being alive. Call the dentist if her gums are swollen or bleeding just to be on the safe side.

Some pregnant women experience hemorrhoids during the second trimester. Others begin to notice varicose veins. Likewise, women often continue to suffer indigestion, constipation, and heartburn, as in the first trimester. The second trimester also brings with it back pain as the growing fetus puts added pressure on mama's back. Other mothers notice their face and/or belly gets dark due to added skin pigmentation caused by pregnancy hormones.

Your partner should continue to eat a highly nutritious, healthy, and balanced diet (see **Chapter One**). She will also benefit from regular light exercises, such as a slow-paced 30-minute walk or some prenatal yoga. It is safe to have sex during the second trimester as long as you don't put pressure on your partner's growing stomach. Don't be worried if she begins to feel mild contractions in the second trimester. This is normal with some women. If the contractions are painful, are accompanied by heavy bleeding, and do not let up even after changing positions or moving, call the doctor immediately.

Prenatal Visits

Second-trimester prenatal visits are fairly standard, so there is nothing to worry about! One of the most important visits during the second trimester is the ultrasound. Your partner will have her first ultrasound (also known as a sonogram) in week 20. The ultrasound is a very important visit for mother and baby. This is when doctors check how many babies you are having. The sonogram will also give the doctors a fairly accurate reading of your due date.

The doctor will be able to pick up any complications in the womb during the ultrasound. For example, if the fetus is not growing as fast as it should be or if there are parts of the fetus that are not developing properly. The sonogram will also be able to pick up potential genetic abnormalities. If this happens, your doctor will refer you for further genetic testing.

Another way in which doctors verify that the fetus is growing properly is by checking the fundal height of the uterus. The fundal height is measured starting at the pubic bone to the top of the uterus. The fundal height should increase to meet the average size of the fetus' weekly growth. Too large or too big tells your practitioner that there is a problem.

Between weeks 24 and 28, your partner will also take a glucose screening. This is to check for the onset of gestational diabetes. Gestational diabetes is very dangerous for both mother and baby. It could result in a larger-than-normal baby being born, leading to a difficult delivery and future health complications for mother and baby.

Your partner will also be given a urine test to check for albumin. Albumin is a protein in the urine that can sometimes act as a symptom of preeclampsia (also known as toxemia). Other routine tests are blood pressure tests and a test to determine the mother's weight. Preeclampsia can typically occur anytime from the 20th week of pregnancy up until birth. In rare cases, it can also be seen in postpartum women. Pregnant women with preeclampsia will have high blood pressure and trouble with their lungs, liver, kidneys, or brain.

You will be given the option to screen for chromosomal or genetic birth defects during the second trimester. It is possible to test for these complications in the first trimester, however, these tests are usually more accurate when administered in the second trimester. Your doctor will determine whether you need to carry out these tests and in what trimester, based on your risk factors, your age, and any abnormal results from your first-trimester screening.

The doctor will also ask your partner the following questions:

- Is she sleeping well? What is her sleeping pattern?

- Does she often feel nauseated? Does she often feel light-headed or dizzy?
- Does she often feel aches and pains, such as heartburn, headaches, or constipation?
- Has she begun to feel contractions?
- Has she begun to feel the baby moving?
- Is she experiencing normal second-trimester vaginal spotting or bleeding?
- Does she eat a healthy diet and take her prenatal vitamins?

Planning For Childbirth

Childbirth is a natural miracle, albeit a chaotic one. To minimize the chaos, doctors generally like to plan childbirth before it happens. Gone are the days of running around trying to find as many towels as possible and boil as much hot water as you can! Plus, like everything else, having a solid plan in place will help you feel more in control of what can be an overwhelming experience.

The best way to plan for birth is to speak with your doctor or OB-GYN during your partner's regular checkups. Many parents often have questions about childbirth pop into their heads during the everyday routine. I encourage you to write these questions down on your phone or a notepad so you remember them during your partner's next checkup.

Planning for childbirth typically begins after the first trimester. Doctors always want to make sure that the fetus passes the first trimester because this is the period when most pregnant women suffer miscarriages.

After the first trimester is completed, you and your partner can pack your hospital bag. Place the hospital bag at a handy location ready to grab on your way to the hospital. Many men like to feel prepared and keep one in the car too. In the excitement of labor, you may forget to pick up your hospital bag (I know a guy whose partner wasn't too happy when he picked up his gym bag filled with smelly old gym clothes instead) so keeping a spare one in the car will be a life-saver.

PACKING YOUR HOSPITAL BAG

1. Here is a handy list of things you need to pack in your hospital bag (tick as you go):
2. Photo identification.
3. Insurance details.
4. Details of your midwife or OB-GYN.
5. Details of your doula, if you have one.

6. Mobile phone and charger (or power bank).

7. Debit/credit cards.

8. Healthy snacks for mother and you.

9. Water and healthy drinks for mother and you.

10. Newborn baby diapers (about fifty disposable diapers. If you are using reusable diapers, take about twenty reusables and twenty disposables in case of emergencies.)

11. Baby clothes to last ten days in the hospital. (Choose clothes that are appropriate for the weather in your area).

12. Sunshade for your car to protect your baby's skin from the harsh sunlight.

13. Newborn baby formula to feed the baby for a week. (Even if your partner decides to breastfeed, take some baby formula in case breastfeeding does not work out).

14. Breast pump.

15. Nipple brushes.

16. Newborn baby bottles and bottle brushes.

17. Two changes of comfortable clothes for your overnight stay.

18. A few comfortable maternity clothes for your partner.

19. Nursing bra and breast pads for the nursing mother.

20. Nursing pillow for the nursing mother.

21. Comfortable maternity shoes for your partner.

22. Toiletries, such as toothpaste, soap, lotion, toothbrushes, and so on.

23. A few baby blankets.

24. Newborn baby bibs.

25. Pacifiers for your baby.

26. Burp cloths.

27. Five packs of disposable wipes (or washable washcloths and mild baby detergent).

28. Changing pad.

29. Nipple cream for the nursing mother.

30. A pillow and a blanket for catching a few hours of sleep at the hospital.

31. Something to entertain you in the hospital, such as a tablet or book.

Getting Your Baby Home

There are many baby carriers available but for a newborn baby you must choose carefully. Check your national and local laws about baby car seats, baby carriers, and baby prams to ensure you comply with regulations and that you purchase ones that meet governmental regulations. In some cases, you may be legally required to get an official car seat inspection from an engineer before you can use it.

You should install the carrier into your car a few months before your partner is due for labor. It takes a lot of practice for you to perfect fitting the car seat securely, so keep on trying until you get it right. Leave the car seat in your car in the third trimester so that you have it ready for bringing your baby back home. Place a baby carrier in the car seat too.

You can go to the car to get the car seat and baby carrier whenever you need them. If you don't want to use a baby carrier, then place a foldable baby pram in the trunk of your car.

In the second trimester, you should begin to plan your childbirth with your healthcare practitioner. This is called a "birth plan." Some people like to wait until their third trimester, but if you start in the second trimester, you get enough time to plan well and to make changes if you want. Birth plans are flexible because, as mentioned, childbirth is chaotic. What happens if your partner's birth is taking longer for example? Or if your partner needs a cesarean? I recommend you have a birth plan for when your birth goes according to plan and a birth plan that covers labor complications. Your midwife/doctor will try their best to follow your birth plan as closely as possible.

Your Birth Plan

Your birth plan will include instructions to the hospital, such as:

- What birth position your partner prefers.
- Whether you want a water birth.
- Whether you want a home birth or hospital birth.
- Whether your partner wants a medicated or unmedicated birth.
- Whether your partner wants a natural birth or a C-section. What to do if your partner wants a C-section.
- Whether your partner wants a doula to give you emotional, physical, and educational support.
- What pain medications your partner wants to take during birth, for example, epidurals.
- What kind of environment you want to create during birth, such as aromatherapy and candles.
- What special requests you have if your partner needs a cesarean surgery.
- What happens if the baby needs a forceps-delivery or vacuum-assisted delivery.
- What happens if the mother gets too tired to push.

- How your partner wants to stay hydrated during the delivery, such as IV drips, ice chips, or water.
- Whether your partner wants to breastfeed your baby.
- If your partner wants to breastfeed your baby, whether she wants a lactation consultant to help her with the first breastfeeding experience. If you both choose a home birth, how you plan to get to the hospital as quickly as possible if complications happen.
- Whether your partner wants skin-to-skin contact with your baby immediately after birth.

You will both need to discuss your birth plan with your doctor and with the labor and birth department of your hospital. They will let you know what parts of your birth plan are unnecessary and which ones cannot be accommodated by the hospital. For example, the hospital may not have a lactation consultant. The hospital will, nonetheless, try its best to accommodate you and to make you feel comfortable by following your birth plan (as long as everything on the list is achievable and does not harm either the mother or baby).

CHAPTER FIVE

What To Expect In The Third Trimester

Did You Know?

Seahorses are the only male animals in the world who get pregnant.

THE THIRD TRIMESTER CAN be the most nerve-wracking. The baby is real now! You can feel and see them kicking, stretching, and moving in your partner's belly. Every day your partner's belly grows bigger and the weeks seem to be speeding by. Hopefully, by now you have made all the preparations you need to make for your baby's arrival.

Your partner is relying on you more. She cannot bend to tie her shoelaces or get off the sofa on her own. And yes, while it may be secretly comical to watch a grown woman struggle to get off a sofa, your best course of action might be to help her when she needs your help. If you are feeling nervous about whether you are ready or will make a great father, then simply remind yourself that all fathers feel this way. You will be fine!

Finally, don't be surprised if you notice you start to experience sympathy pains (couvade syndrome). I know it is often shown as a joke on television (and it is a little bit funny), but some men do experience pain during their partner's pregnancy. Also known as sympathetic pregnancy, sympathy pains will typically see you having the same pains that mimic your partner's pain, like gas, bloating, irritability, weight gain, and nausea. Some men even begin to hold on to their bellies as a pregnant woman does! Do not worry if this happens to you. It will pass soon.

Fetal Growth

By **week twenty-eight** the baby's eyes will partially open. Your baby will now be able to open and close its eyes. The eyes will be able to react to light now. Your baby's central nervous system continues to develop. It can now control your baby's temperature and allows your baby to breathe in rhythm. Your baby is about the size of a lettuce measuring about 10 inches and weighing about 2.5 pounds.

By **week twenty-nine** your baby will start moving a lot, stretching, kicking, and grasping. Your baby's kicks will feel stronger every time. Most of its organs will have fully developed, apart from the lungs. The lungs will not have developed enough to allow your baby to survive outside the womb on its own. Your baby is now the size of a butternut squash, measuring about 10.5 inches and weighing about 3 pounds (about 48 ounces).

Your baby's eyes can now open fully by **week thirty**. The hair will now be growing rapidly on your baby's head. Your partner may now even be able to feel it hiccupping. Fat keeps accumulating on the body, making the skin less wrinkly. The lanugo now starts to disappear in preparation for birth. Your baby is now about the size of a cabbage, measuring about 10.5 to 10.75 inches.

Your baby will now begin to gain weight very quickly from **week thirty-one**. Bones will begin to harden except the bones of the skull which need to stay soft so it is easy for your baby to pass through the birth canal during birth. Your baby will now drink a lot of the amniotic fluid and begin peeing it back out (which is a little gross). The brain also continues to develop with your baby now about the size of a coconut, measuring about 11 inches and weighing about 3.75 pounds.

Your baby's eyes are developed enough to react to light by **weeks thirty-two** to **thirty-three**. As well as a full head of hair, your baby has now developed eyelashes and eyebrows (don't be surprised if your baby is not born with a full head of hair, this is also normal). From now until a few weeks before birth, your baby will turn upside down, standing on its head to prepare for birth. Many babies will even flip back and forth a few times before birth. Toenails will also now be fully formed.

Your healthcare practitioner will check to ensure your baby is standing on its head and ready for birth since babies born with feet or buttocks first often see birth complications. Between **weeks thirty-two** and **thirty-three**, your baby will grow from about 11 inches to about 12 inches.

By **weeks thirty-four** and **thirty-six**, the vernix caseosa will begin thickening in preparation for birth. The lungs will continue to develop too. It will now start producing surfactant, which helps your baby to breathe their first breaths without the air sacs sticking to each other. Your baby is about the size of a romaine lettuce and is now at the length that they will be when born. They are settling into the pelvis, getting ready for birth. Your baby is now measuring between 12.5 inches and 13 inches, weighing about 6 pounds.

Your baby is getting fatter and ready for birth by **weeks thirty-seven** and **thirty-eight**. The brain is still growing and the liver is almost developed. Meconium is now building up in their intestines. Your partner will now begin to notice signs of labor and can even go into labor at this point. Your baby's crown-rump length will now measure around 13.25 inches.

Your pregnancy is at full term by **week thirty-nine**. The lungs are still producing surfactants. Your baby is the size of a mini-watermelon, around 15-16 inches

Week forty is the final week of pregnancy. Some women do not go into labor until weeks forty-one or forty-two and if your baby has not arrived by week forty-two, a cesarean may be performed to birth the baby. At this stage, having gone the full term your baby will be the size of a pumpkin, measuring between 18 to 20 inches and weighing between 6 and 9 pounds.

Mother's Health and Body

Your partner will begin to nap a lot because she is constantly tired. In addition, things are disturbing her from getting a good night's sleep. She might begin to suffer from restless leg syndrome, constant urination, leg cramps, baby moving at night, strange dreams, heartburn, and nasal congestion, all, or some of which are keeping her up at night.

She will very likely become highly emotional too because she is dealing with the fact that the baby is coming soon. I encourage you to talk to her about how you are both feeling about your baby's arrival. It will be very cathartic for both of you. In addition, she will begin to retain a lot of water, with parts of her body becoming puffy, including her face and her hands. This is no cause for alarm except if the swelling on her feet and hands becomes very extreme, accompanied by other signs of preeclampsia, including blurred vision, headache, pain in the belly, and dizziness.

During the third trimester, the mother's "nesting instinct" kicks in. The nesting instinct is involuntarily just like sympathy pains. Mothers typically nest in the third trimester, preparing the home for the baby's arrival just as a mother bird prepares a comfortable nest for her soon-to-be-laid eggs. All this means is she will begin to clean a lot and compulsively do things to make the house ready for your baby's arrival.

She will need plenty of back and foot rubs since the growing baby is now putting pressure on both body parts. Finally, as a word of advice, this might be the point in pregnancy when she suddenly blames you for doing this to her. She is tired, restless, sleepy, in pain, burnt out from the past nine months or so, and just wants to go back to normal, so you might come into the line of fire. In this situation, I have no advice for you. After all, you laid this bed!

If your partner is struggling to sleep, there are ways to relieve her symptoms. Speak to your doctor about her particular ailments for advice on how to improve and lessen these symptoms. Unless told not to by your doctor, your partner should still do light exercises even during the third trimester. She should simply avoid any exercise that can bring harm to her and the baby.

These include exercises like hot yoga/pilates, high-impact water sports like skiing, contact sports and/or exercises where her stomach may be hit like boxing, exercises where she has to lie on her back, and scuba diving. One exercise she can still do is have sex, but many women in their third trimester are often too fatigued and uncomfortable to have sex.

By the third trimester, you will need to call the doctor immediately if she notices any blood as this is a very bad sign. A pink or red blood-tinged mucus discharge is fine, however.

Prenatal Visits

She will need to go in for prenatal visits about once or twice monthly during the third trimester. This frequency will increase to once weekly by week 36. Doctors are always extra careful so that they can catch any complications as soon as possible.

Your doctor will also brief you on all the symptoms of complications to watch out for so you can call them right away if you notice any. One of the most important symptoms is a baby that stops moving or is moving much less than normal. This could be very serious, so inform your doctor immediately if this happens.

In addition, your partner will be given some vaccinations during the third trimester to protect her and the baby from common third-trimester infections. If your doctor discovers that your baby has still not moved into the head-first position by week 36, they will attempt to manipulate your partner's stomach to switch the baby the right way. If this is still unsuccessful, your partner will be booked for a C-section delivery.

The last few months of your pregnancy are your chance to discuss all your labor expectations with your doctor and your hospital. If your insurance will be covering the birth, then you need to ensure that your insurance does indeed cover all the birth options you chose.

Lastly, don't be afraid to take classes to prepare you to be a father. Taking them with your partner is also a sure-fire way to bond together before your baby arrives. Many first-time fathers often recommend birth classes because it really prepares you for the organized chaos that is a baby's birth. After all, you don't want to be in the doctor's way when he is trying to deliver your baby. It might get slightly annoying!

Your doctor will be eager to speak with you about the signs of labor to prepare you for the baby's arrival. Once you know what to expect, you can make your way to the hospital once the baby is ready to meet the world.

Going Into Labor

Signs of you will notice when your partner is nearing labor are:

- Her stomach may "drop", positioned lower than they have been during the pregnancy. This occurs when the baby changes its position to prepare for birth.
- She begins to dilate, meaning that the end of her uterus, called her cervix, begins to open.
- She begins effacement, which is when her cervix begins to thin, shorten and soften in preparation for birth.
- She begins to feel stronger Braxton-Hicks contractions more frequently. Braxton-Hicks contractions are

her body's way of preparing her for real contractions. That is why they are not as painful. Nevertheless, it is common for women in their third trimester to confuse them for real labor contractions.

- She may begin to have more frequent diarrhea, gas, and cramping as well as a constant backache.

The most obvious signs of labor are:

- She starts to feel cramps in a pattern, i.e. with the time between each cramp shortening as they go along. These cramps will also be extremely painful – much more painful than Braxton-Hicks contractions. As a general rule of thumb, if they are so painful that she cannot speak, then she is in labor.
- Her water breaks. Often, a woman's water will break after contractions begin.

Planning For The Baby's Arrival

Even though you will have packed your hospital bag(s) and babyproofed your home, there are still some finishing touches to take care of before bringing your baby home.

- Keep your home clean and tidy during the few weeks before labor. You want to bring your newborn to a fresh, clean house, not a house filled with germs and dust!

- Prepare and freeze some nutritious, filling meals beforehand. You and your partner will be getting very little sleep in the next few months and may not have time to cook healthy, nutritious meals. Make meals that can be easily thrown into the oven and warmed up. Your partner will need to eat a varied, balanced diet to keep her breast milk healthy (if she is breastfeeding), to heal from delivery, and to gain her strength back.

- Tell your trusted friends and family that labor is near so they, too, can prepare. You will need to rely on them during the first few months. For example, a friend making you some frozen meals for a few weeks can be a godsend, giving you time to get some much-needed sleep. Please do note that you should not bring family and friends around your baby until it gets its first shots of vaccinations – just to be safe!

- Tell your workplace you will be taking paternity leave.

- Find a pediatrician who will take your baby on as a patient. If you are using health insurance, shop around for one who is covered under your insurance. If you have taxed national healthcare in your country, look for a general practitioner who will take your baby on as a patient.

- Place all your bills on standing orders or direct debit, otherwise, you will very likely forget to pay them.
- Add your baby to your insurance policy(ies).
- Rehome pets temporarily until you are sure your baby is ready to meet your pet.
- Do your own research. While the information in this book aims to be comprehensive and wide-reaching, doing your own research is a great way to feel empowered and ready for your baby. You may have specific questions that apply only to you that have not been covered in this book, for example, so doing your research will go a long way!

CHAPTER SIX

Holding Down The Fort

Did You Know?

*Unlike mothers' soothing voices, dads' voices
tend to stay steady when they're talking to
their children. They pretty much talk to their
kids like they talk to adults. In doing so, dads
are giving their young kids a "conversational
bridge" to the outside world.*

THE HIGH STRESS OF childbirth is over and you have finally brought your baby home. It is beautiful. Your partner is knocked out and you are tired too! But your job as a father is not even halfway done! In fact, I hate to burst your bubble and tell you this, but you will have this for many more years to come. We can't cover this in just one chapter (or even one book), so this chapter will cover the next two months, which are the first two months of your baby's life.

Maybe I will tell you what's next in my forthcoming books... let me know if you're interested in your book review!

I want to be honest with you, as this book was written to prepare you for every possibility. I don't want to pretend that pregnancy and childbirth is a stroll through a bed of roses as others describe, so the first thing I will mention is your health.

Now, this might seem counterintuitive since the baby and your partner are the most important people here. While this is true, you must also realize that your family relies on you and needs you desperately now. If you are not in good health then they, too, will struggle. Don't be tempted to put your health on the backburner to take care of your baby and your partner. This is what friends and family are for (see **Chapter One** to remind yourself of the ways in which you should take care of your health and manage your stress).

After your baby is born, both you and your partner will need to watch out for symptoms of postpartum depression. In the United States, about 11 to 20 percent of every 600,000 mothers suffer from postpartum depression (Lehnardt, 2017). In fact, the true number could be higher (Lehnardt, 2017).

Approximately 10% of new fathers also suffer postpartum depression (Langdon, 2021). If your partner has postpartum depression, you also have a 50% chance of developing it yourself (Langdon, 2021). PPD can last for months and years and can affect your ability to take care of your baby.

If you notice the symptoms of depression in yourself or your partner, call your doctor immediately. Signs of depression are lethargy, no interest in anything, personality change, deriving no pleasure from anything, feeling very sad, anxiety, trouble concentrating, and more. Your doctor will speak to you and your partner about PPD before you leave the hospital.

Having depression does not make you a failure as a father. It is completely normal. With the help of your doctor and your friends and family, you will get through it!

Taking Care Of The Baby

The baby is finally home and it seems to only breathe, sleep, poop, and eat. It can't be much trouble, right? You just feed it and change it and everything should carry on as normal. I wish I could live in this fantasy!

Feeding

Firstly, newborn babies eat between every two and three hours. So that means you have to be up every two to three hours during the night to feed your baby. Even if your baby is asleep, you need to wake them up to eat. Your baby may not like this and will let you know in no uncertain terms never to do it again. When you repeat the same thing the next night, your baby will be so pissed off at you, it will scream bloody murder.

For the first two days, your baby needs about half an ounce of milk per feeding. Then, this will increase to one to two ounces. In week two, you will need to up this amount to two to three ounces. This will then increase to three to four ounces by the first month, ending up at four to five ounces by the second month.

Do not wait for your baby to begin crying before feeding it. If your baby starts crying it means they got too hungry. This is bad because then you will have to first soothe your baby before they will then accept the nipple or bottle. Instead, give them food every two to four hours. If they take it then they are hungry. If they reject it, try again in an hour. You can also watch out for signs of hunger, including lip licking, being fussy, sucking on everything, mouth opening, rooting (where the baby moves around the head, jaw, and mouth, looking for a nipple), and placing the hand in the mouth.

Be careful not to overfeed your baby, especially if bottle feeding. I would advise you slightly underfeed your baby rather than overfeed because overfeeding can lead to your baby having painful gas or vomiting. If you underfeed slightly, you can simply feed your baby with more frequency to make up for it. Sometimes, babies want to keep feeding because sucking on something comforts them. A pacifier after feeding will take care of this need perfectly! (If your baby is breastfeeding, introduce pacifiers around week three or four so your baby can get used to your partner's nipple without getting the two confused.)

Colic

Colic can start as early as a few weeks once your baby is born, although it typically affects babies three months or older. Colic is when your baby just won't stop crying for no reason. It doesn't need to be changed or burped or fed or bathed or sleep. Some doctors theorize that colic happens because the baby misses the familiarity and coziness of the womb and is processing the trauma of childbirth.

Colic can be very damaging to parents' mental health because your baby does not stop crying for hours on end. The best way to deal with it is to both take turns soothing your baby while the other person takes a break, perhaps going for a quick walk or just listening to some music. Colic can make you very, very frustrated, so I cannot stress enough the importance of taking breaks! The best way to deal with it is to create a routine of relaxing activities for the baby when they start crying. Soon, the familiarity and comfort of the routine will break them out of their crying.

Things like giving them a warm bath and then a baby massage could greatly help in calming them back to sleep. You can also bathe your baby and then spend some time in skin-to-skin contact. Skin-to-skin contact is a very important method for bonding with your baby. Babies need to feel that contact to feel emotionally close and bonded to you. In addition, the warmth from your body also soothes them. Plus, your baby is better able to smell your natural scent, get to know you, and feel comforted in the process.

Babies like to be sung to and rocked back and forth during skin-to-skin contact. It is useful to remember that your baby is like an alien on Earth. Everything is strange to him but your voice and your scent. At this age, babies cannot see at a distance past 12 inches. He may recognize your face, but he is still reliant on voice and scent while his eyesight and brain develop. So, the best way to communicate with him is through skin contact and speaking/singing. Luckily, these two methods are also great for bonding with him.

If your baby has had his first round of vaccinations, you can bundle him uptight (if it is cold) or make sure he is well-protected from the sun and the heat (if it is hot) and take him for a walk. The new sights and smells will distract him and stop the crying. However, babies are greatly overwhelmed at this age (remember he is still an alien) so a short walk is fine for now.

Vaccinations

Your baby will receive Hepatitis B (HepB) vaccine (first dose) after birth. Then, she will receive the following vaccinations during the first two months after birth:

- Hepatitis B (HepB) (second dose).
- Polio (IPV) (first dose).
- Diphtheria, whooping cough, and tetanus (DTaP) (first dose).
- Haemophilus influenzae Type B Disease (Hib) (first dose).
- Rotavirus (RV) (first dose).
- Pneumococcal disease (PCVI3) (first dose) (CDC, 2020).

Your baby may have a rash or feel some pain after the vaccines, but these go away pretty quickly. Speak with your pediatrician about the vaccines and how to take care of your baby following his vaccinations.

Bathing Your Newborn Baby

Do not be anxious about bathing your baby for the first time. Once you know the steps to follow, you will do great at it! Plus, you only need to bathe your baby about three times a week (to avoid dry skin). As long as you clean their diaper area thoroughly every time you change her, she will be clean and healthy. (You will need to change your baby's diaper every two to three hours or as needed. Change it regularly even when not soiled, to avoid nappy rash. If you do not know how to change a diaper, simply ask a nurse at the hospital who will be more than happy to demonstrate for you.)

To bathe your baby:

- Wait for their umbilical cord stump to fall off. In the meantime, give them sponge baths using a baby sponge and very little mild baby soap, rubbing them down one body part at a time while she is wrapped comfortably and warmly in a baby towel.
- Once the umbilical cord falls off after a few weeks, gather your soap, shampoo, hooded towel, sponge, and rinsing cup all together near the baby bathtub. Keep the room warm.
- Fill the bathtub with two inches of warm, body temperature water.
- Support your baby's head with your left hand (or right hand if you are a leftie) and place your baby feet first into the water. Keep their head above water at all times.
- Use your other hand to wash their body with the water and a little bit of soap. Pour some warm water on them regularly to keep them soothed and warm.

- Wash their face using just a washcloth and warm water.
- Wash their hair with a drop of baby shampoo, ensuring to avoid their eyes. Keep a wet washcloth nearby to clean out their eyes in case some shampoo gets in.
- Take your baby out of the tub, then dry him.
- Moisturize your baby with baby lotion and moisturize their hair with baby oil, combing it gently.

Sleep

Newborn babies sleep for about fourteen to eighteen hours a day. They need to sleep to grow and put on weight for survival but they will not sleep for long intervals at a time for at least a few months, so that means they will be awake every few hours. When your baby is awake, you will be awake because she will let you know that she is awake. Newborn babies do not like to be left alone and will cry to receive comfort, soothing, contact, feeding, changing, or whatever else they need.

You will become sleep-deprived very quickly if you are bottle-feeding your baby. The best way to deal with it is to sleep while your baby is asleep. Another great way is to let family and friends come over to feed your baby during the night once in a while so that you can get a full night's sleep.

While it might be tempting to be angry at your beautiful innocent baby sleeping sweetly while you are about to drop from your saggy and dark under-eye circles, getting angry is not going to give you the sleep you need! Revenge is a dish best served cold, so I suggest waiting until your baby is at least eighteen years old to pay them back. Then you can think of sweet, sweet revenge that will make it all worth it. If you are not predisposed to evil, however, I suppose your love for your baby will be enough to keep you persevering.

Tummy Time

Newborns cannot hold their heads up because the neck and shoulder muscles are still quite weak. To strengthen these muscles, they will need to practice using them during tummy time. Tummy time is the time you set aside daily to place your baby on his tummy rather than on his back. When you place a newborn on their tummies, they can hold their head and shoulders up.

You should incorporate two to three tummy time sessions per day for your baby for one to two minutes. The amount of time for each tummy time will increase as your baby grows older. At one month old, this figure should go up to three to five minutes. At two months old, tummy time should last between 10 and 20 minutes each time

97

and you can even have it more often to help your baby get swole! Or, if you are not into swole babies, to strengthen their neck and shoulder muscles.

Don't do tummy time after a meal. The best time to do it is after your baby wakes up reinvigorated from a nap or after you have just changed your baby's diaper. Tummy time is also a great way to bond with your baby and spend some skin-to-skin contact as you can place your baby on your chest, supporting them with one hand.

During this time, you should talk to or sing to your baby. You can even read to them or play with a few toys with her. Anything to stimulate their mind and improve their developing brain. If you do not want to spend tummy time having skin-to-skin contact, you can lay a rug on the floor for your baby, spending time on the floor with your baby too.

Tummy time is also used to avoid a flat head. If you have ever noticed a person who seems to have a flat spot at the back of their head, it is because they were left on their backs too long as babies causing their still soft skull to change shape. With tummy time, you can avoid this problem by giving your baby's skull a break regularly.

Taking Care Of Your Partner

Your partner will need your continued care postpartum - especially during the first few months after pregnancy. Not only has their body been through one of the most traumatic things it ever will, she still has to take care of the little bundle of joy at the same time.

To support her during her healing, go shopping regularly for healthy foods to speed up her healing. Draw her baths and give her massages often. Offer to spend time with the baby, so she can catch some much-needed sleep. Be gentle and patient even when her hormones may cause her to act moody or angry. Reassure her that she is still beautiful and you love her even if her body has seen dramatic changes after pregnancy.

You should also keep the house clean and tidy because a dirty, untidy house will affect her mood drastically (not to mention affect your baby's health negatively).

Carving Out A Work-Life Balance

Depending on your country, you may have to go back to work sooner than later. This can be a very difficult transition for the whole family, but it is a doable one. Your partner has learned to rely on you and may find it difficult doing everything now that you are away. Plus, you may feel that you would rather be home bonding with your baby than at work. Often, fathers feel guilty for leaving their newborns at home while they are at work. These are all legitimate feelings that you may have, but you need to remind yourself that you also need to work to provide financially for your family.

Besides, there are ways to carve out a healthy work-life balance. This includes leaving work as soon as your work-day is over, no matter how much responsibility you have, and refusing to answer phone calls or emails until you are back at work. It can also mean taking days off when you can and using up unused holidays. If you had time to spend with your extended family and friends before the baby's arrival, you may have to use that time now to spend with your baby.

Your priorities now are very different. Your baby now comes first. If you have a good relationship with your friends and family, they will understand.

Final Words

By now, you know what fatherhood entails. You are armed with knowledge on how to undertake this wonderful new endeavor. Changing a baby is now demystified for you and, hopefully, you no longer feel alien from the process of fetal development.

Your partner is starting to show now and you have begun accompanying her to prenatal visits. There is so much to do to prepare for fatherhood and time is ticking. This is not to say that you are in a rush or you are anxious! Rather, you are at peace and you are excited to bring your little bundle of joy home.

A word of caution before that day when your baby finally arrives in the world. Babies are tiny! Every new father I have spoken to has told me they couldn't believe how small babies are. Well, they are! Even though babies are getting bigger, your baby will be able to wrap its entire hands around just a quarter of your index finger. I have had two children and am still in awe when I see a newborn baby. The miracle of life truly is a beauty and I am honored to say that I have guided you through this process.

You are now ready to begin this new journey into fatherhood, becoming one of the billions of fathers who have done it before you. This doesn't make it any less special. It just means that you will try your hardest to be the best ever father, out-fathering all those other fathers who thought they had fatherhood down! And I am sure that if there ever was a "World's Best Father" endurance contest, you would win hands down!

It is now time to put down this book, take a quick break, and then pick up your mantle once more! There are diapers to be changed!

FIRST TIME DAD

Resources

American Council On Exercise. (2014, October 7). Top 10 Benefits Of Exercise. Ace Fitness. https://www.acefitness.org/education-and-resources/lifestyle/blog/5107/top-10-benefits-of-stretching/.

American Pregnancy Association. (2021).Creating Your Birth Plan. American Pregnancy Association. https://americanpregnancy.org/healthy-pregnancy/labor-and-birth/birth-plan/.

American Pregnancy Association. (2021). Depression During Pregnancy. American Pregnancy Association.

https://americanpregnancy.org/healthy-pregnancy/pregnancy-health-wellness/depression-during-pregnancy/.

BellyBelly. (2021, March 18). 15 Great Ways To Support Her During Pregnancy. BellyBelly. https://www.bellybelly.com.au/men/15-great-ways-to-support-your-partner-during-pregnancy/.

Bhattacharjee, D. (2018, July 26). How Many Calories To Consume During Pregnancy. First Cry Pregnancy. https://parenting.firstcry.com/articles/how-much-calories-to-consume-during-pregnancy/.

Bradford, E.L. (2021, March 22). Couvade Syndrome (Sympathetic Pregnancy). Baby Center. https://www.babycenter.com/pregnancy/relationships/strange-but-true-couvade-syndrome-sympathetic-pregnancy_10364940.

Bykofsky, M. (2020, September 25). Babyproofing Your House: A Checklist For Every Room. Parents. https://www.parents.com/baby/safety/babyproofing/babyproofing-your-home-from-top-to-bottom/.

CDC. (2021). What Vaccines Will My Baby Get? CDC. https://www.cdc.gov/vaccines/parents/by-age/months-1-2.html.

Chval, L. (2017, March 8). First Trimester Down, Still Waiting For That Pregnancy Glow. Chicago Tribune. https://www.chicagotribune.com/lifestyles/health/sc-i-feel-lousy-in-my-first-trimester-he

Dr. Y. (2021, October 18). Successful C-Sections In Pre-Colonial Africa: Surgery In Bunyoro Kingdom. Afro Legends. https://afrolegends.com/2021/08/18/successful-c-sections-in-pre-colonial-africa/.

Family Doctor. (2019, June 3). Changes In Your Body During Pregnancy: Third Trimester. Family Doctor. https://familydoctor.org/changes-in-your-body-during-pregnancy-third-trimester/.

Heath, K. (2017, September 21). 54 Unique Women Facts. Fact Retriever. https://www.factretriever.com/women-facts.

Hopkins Medicine. (2021). The Second Trimester. Hopkins Medicine. https://www.hopkinsmedicine.org/health/wellness-and-prevention/the-second-trimester.

Jain, S. (2020, October 29). How Often And How Much Should Your Baby Eat? https://www.healthychildren.org/English/ages-stages/baby/feeding-nutrition/Pages/How-Often-and-How-Much-Should-Your-Baby-Eat.aspx.

Jennings, K. (2021, June 21). 11 Best Foods To Boost Your Brain And Memory. Healthline. https://www.healthline.com/nutrition/11-brain-foods.

Jones, B. (2020, October). Colic In Babies. Family Doctor. https://familydoctor.org/condition/colic/.

Kinsella, M.T. & Monk, C. (2013, July 14). Impact Of Maternal Stress, Depression & Anxiety On Fetal Neurobehavioral Development. *Clin Obstet Glynecol.* 52(3), pp. 425-40. https://www.ncbi.nlm.nih.gov/pmc/articles/PMC3710585/.

Langdon, K. (2022). Statistics Of Postpartum Depression. Postpartum Depression. https://www.postpartumdepression.org/resources/statistics/.

Lehnardt, K. (2017, April 12). 73 Interesting Pregnancy Facts. Fact Retriever. https://www.factretriever.com/interesting-pregnancy-facts.

Linton, A. (2021, October 20). Don't Become A Parent Until You've Hit These Money Milestones. The Balance. https://www.thebalance.com/money-milestones-before-having-kids-4144742.

Marple, K. (2019, March 22). Fetal Development Week By Week. Baby Center. https://www.babycenter.com/pregnancy/your-baby/fetal-development-week-by-week_10406730.

Martin, L.T., McNamara, M.J., Milot, S.A. et al. (2007, November). The Effects Of Father Involvement During Pregnancy On Receipt Of Prenatal Care And Maternal Smoking. *Matern Child Health J.* 11 (6), pp.595-602. https://pubmed.ncbi.nlm.nih.gov/17557201/.

Mayo Clinic. (2022). Depression (Major Depressive Disorder. Mayo Clinic. https://www.mayoclinic.org/diseases-conditions/depression/symptoms-causes/syc-20356007.

Mayo Clinic Staff. (2021, April 13). Pregnancy Nutrition: Foods To Avoid During Pregnancy. Mayo Clinic. https://www.mayoclinic.org/healthy-lifestyle/pregnancy-week-by-week/in-depth/pregnancy-nutrition/art-20043844.

Migala, J. (2021, August 9). 20 Foods That Give You All-Day Energy. Livestrong. https://www.livestrong.com/article/13767246-foods-that-give-you-energy/.

OASH. (2019, April 1). Infertility. Women's Health. https://www.womenshealth.gov/a-z-topics/infertility.

Pampers. (2020, April 9). How To Bathe Your Newborn. Pampers. https://www.pampers.com/en-us/baby/newborn/article/your-babys-first-bath.

Pampers. (2021). Pregnancy Calendar. Pampers. https://www.pampers.com/en-us/pregnancy/pregnancy-calendar.

Raising Children. (2021). The Australian Parenting Website. Raising Children. https://raisingchildren.net.au/.

RL 360. (2021). Top 10 Financial Tips For New Dads. RL 360. https://www.rl360.com/top10/financial-tips-for-new-dads.htm.

Rossiter, E. (2019, October 18). A Fifth Of Parents Break-Up In The Year After Having A Baby. Good To Know. https://www.goodto.com/wellbeing/relationships/relationship-news/break-up-after-baby-513710.

Safe To Sleep. (2022). Babies Need Tummy Time. Safe To Sleep. https://safetosleep.nichd.nih.gov/safesleep-basics/tummytime.

Sinrich, J. (2020, June 5). Pregnancy Nutrition Chart: 33 Essential Nutrients For Pregnant Women. What To Expect. https://www.whattoexpect.com/pregnancy/diet/pregnancy-nutrition-chart/.

Stork OTC. (2021). 6 Nutritional Recommendations For Men Trying To Conceive. Stork OTC. https://www.storkotc.com/blog/6-nutritional-recommendations-for-men-trying-to-conceive/.

Top Line MD. (2021). 7 Interesting Facts You May Not Know About Pregnancy. Top Line MD. https://www.toplinemd.com/womens-care-of-bradenton/blog/interesting-facts-about-pregnancy/.

Warburton, D.E.R., Nicol, C.W. & Bredin, S.S.D. (2006, March 14). Health Benefits Of Physical Activity: The Evidence. *CMAJ*. 174(6), pp. 801-9. https://www.ncbi.nlm.nih.gov/pmc/articles/PMC1402378/.

WebMD. (2021). Second Trimester Tests During Pregnancy. WebMD. https://www.webmd.com/baby/guide/second-trimester-tests#1.